Crickhowell Yesterday

100 YEARS OF PHOTOGRAPHS

By John Addis

FOREWORD
by
Hon. Mrs. E. S. J. LEGGE-BOURKE, L.V.O.

First published in September, 1992
RE-PRINT MAY, 2002
© D. J. Addis.

ISBN 1 872808 18 2

ACKNOWLEDGEMENTS

I would like to thank the following people for giving permission for their photographs to be reproduced:

Bob Candy, Brian Boddy, Billy Lloyd, Mrs. Anne Usborne, Mrs. Liz Rees, Bill Havard, Mrs. Austin, Mrs. Marion Probert, Mrs. Bron Price, Mrs. Archibald, Mr. Parsons, Mrs. G. Wilcock, Miss Vera Pullen, Mrs. Joan Francis, Mrs. Doris Shellard, Miss Palliser, Mrs. Shân Legge-Bourke, Brian Couzens and Mrs. Mary Way.

I would also like to thank the following in helping to give names and information to the photographs:

Bryn Meale, Ernie Randall, Miss Gladys Jones, Dai Lewis, Roy Morgan, Mervyn Thomas, Dick Thomas, John Preece, Dr. Humphreys, John Williams and Peter Lovesey.

Grateful thanks are extended to Mrs. Ann Lloyd for her time spent doing the typing and to Mr. David Bebb of Gilwern for developing the original glass negatives that comprise so many of the better photographs.

Lastly a very special thank you to Mrs. Connie Allen and Mavis for releasing the "Wizards" work.

Printed in Wales by B&N Printers, Abergavenny

Foreword

I very much welcome and commend this record of Crickhowell's past to you. It contains many photographs of my family and those associated with them. When my ancestor, Sir Joseph Bailey, bought what became Glanusk Park in 1826, he started a relationship between my family and Crickhowell which not only continues to this day but will, I hope, continue for many generations to come. Maybe that when the next version of this book is published in a hundred years' time they will be able to provide some further contribution to its story. I can only hope so!

John Addis has produced a marvellous record for posterity and I have been only too pleased to help in ferreting out memories and people of the past who helped make Crickhowell what it is today.

Hon. Mrs. E. S. J. Legge-Bourke, L.V.O.

Crickhowell
THE GARDEN OF WALES.

CRICKHOWELL

Preface

I would like to thank the author of this book, John Addis, for the many hours he has spent collecting and checking the photographs.

Many people have old photographs tucked away in odd corners of their homes and when they pass away a lot of these bits of local history are lost to future generations.

In this book the author has managed to collect some of these photographs and to name the people, events and locations of the pictures. Crickhowell has changed a lot in my lifetime and some parts have been completely rebuilt. We have lost a War Memorial Hospital, Youth Hostel, Crown Post Office and Sorting Office, Telephone Exchange and Magistrates' Court; and we have built a new High School, Fire Station, Ambulance Station, Health Centre, Residential Home for the Elderly, Re-modelled Primary School and Sheltered Housing Complex.

What does the next 50 years hold in store for Crickhowell?

Brian Couzens B.E.M., J.P.,
Chairman, Crickhowell Community Council.
1991-92

Introduction

I have tried to put together some of the past in old photographs collected by myself, and others loaned to me by inhabitants of Crickhowell. I thank these people for their help, also my wife, Susan, for her understanding and help in putting the book together; without their help it would not have been possible.   Most of the photographs were taken by a grand old man called Mr. Tommy Allen. He was famous for his work in the late nineteenth and early twentieth centuries. Some of his family still live in Crickhowell.

This is produced to delight people and not offend. I have tried to date and name as many people as possible. I am sure you will find it an interesting book, to see how Crickhowell looked long ago.

Crickhowell has been called many beautiful names, like "The Garden of Wales", or "The Glittering Jewel of the Vale", with its distant blue mountains, grassy slopes and craggy cliffs. With its shaded lanes, rolling parklands and sparkling waters, such a variety of character and enchanting prettiness combines to form the Black Mountains and the Brecon Beacons. An early guide, c.1900 describes the ancient stronghold of "Hywel Dda", with its camp on top of a hill known as the "Table Mountain", or by its proper name Craig Hywel (Hywel's Rock) which overlooks this beautiful town.

Hywel Dda was the first ruler to frame a code of laws by which to govern the Welsh. The code included silly little laws such as "Someone to seek a bundle of straw for the King's bed" or the "Court Crier of Silence" who appears to have been like a mediaeval 'chucker out'. An extract from the late Hon. Mabel Bailey guide states that from the top of the Table Mountain a path leads past the "Wern Farm", down a long lane to the top of Llanbedr Road. Where the road joins the lane there is a little wood, which is said to be haunted by a mysterious black dog, which appears to frighten the nervous. She also states that on "Twyn-y-Wlad Farm" near the wood, is a field called Cae-cynta-ceffyl (the first horse's field). For very curious reasons this field stands in the three parishes of Crickhowell, Llanbedr and Llangenny. In the olden days, nobody knew to which parish the tythe belonged, so the Rectors of each parish agreed that every year they would ride a race to the field; the first to arrive would secure the tythe.

The old castle standing in the recreation ground is not the original castle of Hywel Dda. Known as Alisby Castle, it was built in 1272 by the Norman Sir Grimbald Pauncefoot, but seized in 1320 by Roger Mortimer who was thrown into the Tower of London. He escaped with the help of Alisby, who later governed the castle. It is from the birds that built their nest in the remaining towers that the people of Crickhowell get their nickname "Jackdaws".

The Clarence Hall, of which the foundation stone was laid by the Duke of Clarence in 1890, was the first foundation stone in South Wales to be laid by Royalty for a public hall.

Standard Street was so called because it was here that Sir Richard Evans raised his standard, and with three thousand Breconshire men marched to the assistance of Henry Tudor (Henry VII) and shared victory on Bosworth field.

The drinking fountain in the centre of the town was built in memory of Dr. Henry Lucas, who was a much loved person in the town.

ORIGINAL CASTLE, CRICKHOWELL.

The picturesque "Gateway of Porthmawr" was once the entrance to a castellated mansion called Cwrt-y-Carw (The Stag Court) which belonged to a branch of the Herbert family. The gateway is all that remains of the old house.

St. Edmund's Church, is dedicated to St. Edmund, King and Martyr, who was martyred by the Danes 870. The church is cruciform in shape and has a wonderful history.

Thursday is still considered as Market Day. An interesting annual event is Mediaeval Day. Held in July, the High Street is closed to traffic, everyone dresses up in Mediaeval clothing and market stalls are held to raise money for charities.

A little way out of Crickhowell on the right hand side is "Gwernvale", a property which once belonged to the family named Proger. Phillip Proger (who was equerry to James I) was given a pension of sixty pounds for life. It is also the birthplace of George Everest the Surveyor General of India after whom Mount Everest was named. At the entrance to Gwernvale is an ancient burial place.

A little along the Brecon road is a field called Cae-y-Crochenydd or the Potter's field. Tradition says that it was used—as its name implies—to bury strangers in. Here, where the lane turns up the hill by the cottage called Llanvair (Mary's Church) there once stood a chapel, dedicated to the Blessed Virgin. The last remains of this chapel, were removed early in the 19th century to make room for a barn, presumably the one still standing on the left.

In the adjoining field is a mound covered with trees, thought to have been a watch-tower on the old Roman road, Strata Julia, which passes by Llanvair.

I will conclude this brief history of Crickhowell with mention of the bridge, built in approximately 1535, rebuilt in 1706, and widened 1809 when twelve arches were formed on one side and thirteen on the other.

Across the bridge lies Llangattock village. There has always been a friendly rivalry between Crickhowell (Jackdaws) and their neighbours, the Llangattock Mice.

The parishes of Llangattock, Llangenny, Llanbedr, Cwmdu, Tretower and Llangynidr are so closely connected that in thinking of one, you naturally include the other.

The Town and its Traders

1 c.1900. Three Salmons, Bridge Street. The photograph shows the landlord and landlady Mr. & Mrs. John Herbert. The pub is now a private dwelling.

2 c.1888. The lower end of High Street. On the right the Queens Head.

3 *c.*1890. The Swan, Llanbedr Road with Mrs. Jones, Landlady, at the door.

4 The Bear Hotel. Mrs. Amabernethy, the landlady, looking at a "Local Fisherman" sat in a tin tub. The photo was taken about *c.*1900; it appeared in a local newspaper and the caption under said that locals wanted their own fishing and boating on the Usk, but were not allowed, so the next best was this!

5   *c.*1900. Mrs. & Mrs. Davies, proprietors standing outside. The sign over the front says that there is good stabling and accommodation for cyclists at the Corn Exchange.

6   *c.*1900. Looking down Beaufort Street showing the Beaufort Arms, with Mr. & Mrs. Watkins standing outside. The cottage at the end is now the Chemist.

7   1898. The landlady and landlord outside the Vinetree with some of their regulars.

8   Cwmbeth Gate 1892 then a Tollgate and pub, now the Whitehart pub.

9 *c.*1900. The Green as you enter Crickhowell. Semi-detached houses stand there now.
On the left, the cottages in Castle Road were demolished a lot later for the Glan-yr-Afon flats.
The posters on the wall mention the Boer War and Chipperfields Circus.

10 *c.*1910. Williams the Saddlers and the Cambrian Arms.

11   1916. A view of Llangattock and the Horseshoe pub.

12   A very early photograph of Nantyffin Cider Mill, now a Restaurant and Pub. The photograph
was taken off a glass negative produced around 1880.

13 Looking up the High Street in 1949. The car on the right belonged to Mr. George Parum.

14 c.1928. The town centre.

15 1904. Shopping in the High Street. The only real change is that the garage belonging to Latham House has been demolished, and a shop and flats have been built.

16 1889. Looking down Beaufort Street before the Clarence Hall was built.

17 1949. Roadworks in Beaufort Street. The cottage on the left used to be the "Bush Pub". Notice the top of the petrol pump on the right hand side of the photograph.

18 1928. Outside the Bear Hotel. This fine band of gentlemen are making sure you do not forget the Abergavenny Hospital Fete.

19 *c.*1900. The Bevan Memorial, Brecon Road. Victoria Terrace (Ten Houses) is covered in ivy with a large tree standing on the corner.

20 1926. Porthmawr Gateway. Note the shell sign on the right belonging to the garage.

21 *c.*1890. The Beaufort Arms. A good view of the old cottages where now stands the Council Offices.

22 1935. Looking up Silver Lane, now the home of the Library. The small child in the photograph is Mr. Lance Huxley.

23   1897. Looking down Brecon Road from the entrance to Porthmawr Lodge.

24   *c*.1900. A view from the river bridge up New Road.

25 Bell Stores, early *c.*1900. A. F. Wallace Shop is now Jehu's. Mr. Mathews who lived at Herbert Hall was the last person to own the Bell Stores.

26 Bell Stores being demolished early 1930's. Reg Beavis is seen working on the demolition.

27 Shop window of Bell Stores shows an advertising campaign for Macfarlane Langs biscuits.
By the door 7lb of potatoes for one shilling.

28 Watching the troops go by Townsend Boot and Shoe Stores. Now run as an electrical shop.
Photograph was taken before the next door office of Solicitors was built.

29 1940's. Nicholls Grain Stores. Mr. Les Nicholls is seen standing in the doorway.

30 1925. James Isaac Shop.

Overleaf **31-46** Trade advertisements *c*.1900.

The Hon. Sec. of the Crickhowell Improvement
Association will, on receipt of a stamped ad-
dressed envelope, post to any applicant a printed
list of Apartments and Houses to Let.

THE CLYDACH VALLEY, NEAR CRICKHOWELL.

47 Ivy Towers 1920. This was the local hospital which was closed in the 1930s. The hospital had 3 wards. One with 4 beds for men. One with 4 beds for ladies. One private bed. Two beds at the top. The tower was the mortuary. The cottage was the maternity wing with 4 beds. The hospital made their own electricity.

Before becoming the local hospital Ivy Towers was a school and before that a private house.

48 1912. River Bridge. Notice the windows in the cottage next to the Bridgend Inn. A strip of ground between the Inn garden and the river was used by local farmers to wash their sheep.

49 1895. The Clarence Hall. Mr. T. Allen used to operate his business from the shed in the garden.

50 1895. Inside the Clarence Hall. The stage is ready for a performance.

Local Views

51   1930. A view of Llangenny Lane from the Wellsfield before any houses were built.

52   A view of the town taken from the tump in the recreation ground *c.*1900.

53 1950. In this view from the bridge, on your left the old gas works can be seen.

54 1950. A view of the bridge with the Table Mountain in the background.

55 1955. Looking down on Crickhowell. The entrance to the Pregge Farm Estate was then an orchard owned by Mr. Pullen.

56 1930. The Dardy. The union workhouse is seen near the top.

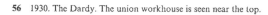

57   1889. The man is seen carrying a yoke, there is a scraper on the monument. He was probably
cleaning up the horse droppings.

58   A snow scene at Llangrwyney 1904.

59 Early *c*.1900 at Llangenny. Pendarren can be seen on the right.

60 Early *c*.1900. Looking down on Cwmdu.

61 1885. View of Crickhowell. Notice the Clarence Hall is not yet built.

62   1970. Aerial view of the town.

63 Pregge Mill at the turn of the century. Part of the old iron wheel can still be seen today.

64 1889. The tollgate at Greenhill (now demolished), it was situated opposite the entrance to Elvicta Estate where the bus shelter now stands.

65 *c.*1900. Llanbedr and the Sugar Loaf mountain.

66 1895. Alisby Castle. The square part of the tower has now partly fallen down and the ivy has been cleaned off.

Buildings

67 Cwrt-y-Gollen House. The estate belonged to the Morgan family and was then passed on to the Davies family who kept it for approximately 150 years. It was bought by the Sandeman family from Dan-y-Parc in 1891 at an auction.

Very sadly it was burnt down when workmen were working there about 1911.

The Military took over in the 1939-45 war when it was used for an American camp. The army formed the Welsh Brigade depot there in 1960, but closed it as a full-time camp in 1986.

It used to have iron entrance gates, curiously fashioned of iron circles riveted together, said to have been made in Llangrwyney Smithy. The gate is now situated at the entrance to the former Dan-y-Parc estate on the Gilwern Road. (Similar gates can be seen at the "Plas", Llangattock.)

68 & 69 Glanusk Park. Built in 1826. The architect was Robert Lugar, who also built Cyfartha Castle. The ground plan is the same as Maeslwch Castle. Glanusk Park House was demolished in 1954. There used to be a life-size statue of Wellington housed there.

70   *c*.1900. Llangattock Park House. Owned by the Duke of Beaufort who was Lord of the Manor.
     The late Duke of Beaufort was said to have been born here.

71   Llangattock Park with the Marconi family visiting (Marconi Electrics.)

72 The last hospital in Crickhowell, demolished in 1970. When a private home it was known as Greenhill House, owned by Mr. Johns. It later became the War Memorial Hospital. Lord Glanusk started an appeal fund in 1918 for it to become a hospital.

73 1920. Dan-y-Castle Chapel.

74   1901. Looking through, Porthmawr gate.

75   A view of the tower.

76 St. Edmonds Church displaying the new copper to the steeple.

77   c.1900. Cwmdu Church. On the right the Six Bells pub, now a cottage.

78   Bethabara Chapel, Bridge Street c.1900. Just under the garden wall of the Bridgend pub, the local farmers used to wash their sheep.

79 The tower of St. Edmonds with the wooden scaffold around, after the oak shingles were taken off and the copper fixed on. A violent storm ripped part of the copper off and it was removed and cedar shingles fixed back in 1964.

80 Interior of St. Edmonds Church before the Lady Chapel c.1900. The Lady Chapel was installed in memory of the 1914/18 war.

INTERIOR PARISH CHURCH, CRICKHOWELL

81   Glan-yr-Afon, Castle Road 1889. Home of Dr. Lucas who has a monument in his memory in
      the High Street. Dr. Lucas's daughter married the 1st Lord Glanusk.
Gencral Curtis lived there after Dr. Lucas, and after The Curtis's a Mr. Williams bought it and then
      sold it to the Convent. It is now owned by the Council and is a block of flats.

82   Gwernvale Manor 1908. The birthplace of Everest, Surveyor General of India who gave his
      name to Mount Everest. Now a private leisure club and hotel.

83   Gliffaes 1909. Now a Country Hotel. Built 1883/5.

84   Pendarren House, Llangenny 1905. Now an Outward Bound Centre.

85   *(opposite)* This building in Bridge Street was a school in the early c.1800. Believed to be the first school in Crickhowell where pupils paid 1 penny in old money to attend. It later became a builder's workshop and has now been developed into a dwelling. Photograph taken in 1970.

Dany Park, Crickhowell. 1631.

86 Dan-y-Parc House 1890. It was sold to a Mr. Kendall at the end of the eighteenth century. In 1856 it was sold to Alfred Crawshay. It was then left to his son-in-law Captain Robert Sandeman in 1890. Demolished in 1956.

87 1896. Llangattock Church and school. The clock has now gone on the school and the Bell has disappeared. Private dwellings now occupy the site.

PROGRAMME OF

PRESENTATION OF AN ADDRESS

TO HIS H.R.H. THE

DUKE OF CLARENCE & AVONDALE

BY THE INHABITANTS OF THE TOWN AND NEIGHBOURHOOD OF CRICKHOWELL, AND

The Laying of the Foundation Stone

OF THE NEW PUBLIC HALL

++ BY H.R.H. ON THE 18TH SEPTEMBER, 1890. ++

There will be a Guard of Honour formed up by C Company of the 1st Breconshire V.R.S.W.B., who will give a Royal Salute on the arrival of the Prince.

H.R.H. will arrive punctually at 11 o'clock and will be received by Councillor E. Gratton Davis and the Chairman, and Secretary, and the Members of the Presentation and Decoration Committee, and by Edward Bowen Evans, Esq., the Chairman of the Directors of the Public Hall Company, and by the Officers of the Company.

The Presentation of the Address will then be made, and the Chairman and Secretary of the Committee will be presented to the Prince, after which the ceremony of laying the foundation stone will take place.

The Chairman of Directors will request H.R.H. to lay the stone with the trowel and mallet which will be presented to him by the Chairman's Sister Miss Evans, and the same will be previously handed to Miss Evans by Mr. E. A. Johnson the Architect.

The Directors, and Architect, and Officers of the Public Hall Company will then be presented to H.R.H.

Those who hold tickets for reserved seats for the Pavilion will be in their places by 10-30.

GOD SAVE THE QUEEN.

88   Programme for the Laying of the Foundation Stone by the Duke of Clarence.

89   His Royal Highness the Duke of Clarence laying the foundation stone in 1890 to the new Clarence Hall. The foundation stone is believed to be the first to be laid by Royalty for a Public Hall in South Wales.

90 1890. This photograph shows the celebration of laying the foundation stone at the Clarence Hall after the crowd had left.
C. Malvern & Sons of Cheltenham were the contractors for the foundations, but not for the main building; they also supplied the foundation stone. The face of the stone was replaced in 1954.

EXTRACTS FROM CONTEMPORARY NEWSPAPERS

91A "A trowel presented, together with an ivory mallet, to his Royal Highness the Duke of Clarence and Avondale, by the Crickhowell Public-hall Company (Limited) on the occasion of his laying the foundation stone of the Public-hall, September, 1890. Both were enclosed in a handsome morocco case, and were supplied by Messrs. Elkington and Co., of Birmingham. His Royal Highness then spread the mortar with the trowel, and the stone being duly lowered into position, the Prince, at the same time tapping the four corners of the stone with the mallet declared it well and truly laid, amid cheers. In the cavity of the stone was placed a sealed bottle containing a copy of Wednesday's *Western Mail*, a five-shilling piece, a half-crown, and a penny bearing the date 1890, and a slip of vellum with the words, 'Crickhowell Public-hall. Foundation stone laid September 18, 1890, by H.R.H. Prince Albert Victor.' Mrs. Gratrex Davies then presented a beautiful gardenia to his Royal Highness, who shook hands with the donor and thanked her for her graceful tribute."

91B "A limited liability venture, under the style of the Crickhowell Public-Hall Company, was registered last week, with a capital of £2,500 in £1 shares, for the purpose of carrying out the work of building. The directors at present acting are Mr. E. B. Evans, Llangattock Park (chairman); Sir Joseph Bailey, Bart., M.P., Mr. R. T. Woosnam, Mr. J. A. Doyle, Mr. D. K. Mason, Mr. Robert Harris, and Mr. S. H. Cowper-Coles. Mr. E. G. Davies is the solicitor, Mr. Irvine Blennerhassett secretary, Mr. E. A. Johnson, of Abergavenny and Newport, architect; the bankers being the National Provincial Bank. A large number of the shares have already been taken, and the others are now being offered to the public.
At the site of the new edifice (kindly granted by Sir Joseph Bailey on a nominal rent) a spacious pavilion had been erected by Messrs. C. Malvern and Son, builders and contractors, Cheltenham, in whose hands the work of preparing the foundations and of providing the stone had been placed pending the acceptance of tenders for building the hall."

1890 — PROPOSED PUBLIC HALL CRICKHOWELL — E. A. Johnson, Architect. Abergavenny & Newport

92 DESCRIPTION OF THE NEW PUBLIC-HALL

"The new Public-hall is being erected by a public company on a site in Beaufort-street, close to the centre of the town, The plans, which have been prepared by Mr. E. A. Johnson, architect of Abergavenny and Newport, show that the building will be in the Renaissance style, with a commanding frontage towards Beaufort-street, opposite the National Provincial Company's banking premises. The elevation will be of a pleasing character, the general aspect being emphasised by a tower, which will form a prominent feature in the design. The hall on the ground floor, which will be approached by means of a nicely ornamented entrance lobby laid with tesselated pavement, will be 75ft. by 40ft., the height from the floor—which will be of wooden blocks—to the most elevated point in the open timber roof being 30ft. The room will be furnished to accommodate about 500 persons. It will be provided with a commodious stage, with dressing-rooms adjoining (convertible into a large supper-room), and there will be as adjuncts the usual retiring rooms. There will also be a caretaker's cottage and armoury for the Volunteers. The walls are to be built of local grey sandstone, with Bath stone dressings. It is estimated that the cost will amount to £2,500, but the contract for building has not yet been let. The company will probably name it the Clarence-hall, in commemoration of the Prince's connection with the building."

93 The Clarence Hall in the process of being built 1891.
The builders for the main super structure were believed to have been Williams & Son, Contractors of Knighton

94 Finished Hall. Completed and opened in 1892 at an approximate cost of £2,500.
The last surviving shareholder was Lord Glanusk (Lord Lieutenant of the County) who died in 1948. Before his death he was largely responsible for the building being offered to the town. He performed the ceremony which celebrated its transference to public ownership.

Events

95 1890. Outside the Bear Hotel. On the left can be seen a large house, where the Conservative Club now stands. The large house was called Ty-Berllan. When demolished the stone was used for the building of the Drill Hall in Castle Road.

96 1890. Looking up the High Street, just before the visit of His Royal Highness the Duke of Clarence. The photograph shows one of many arches erected to celebrate his arrival.

97 The scene on the road A40 centre of Crickhowell shows a celebration arch for the Duke's visit in 1890.

98 Celebration Arch at Porthmawr Gate 1890

99 1890. Putting up the flags and decorations for the visit of His Royal Highness The Duke of Clarence.

100 At that time the market hall had railings across the front. They were bolted to the base of the pillars. The fixings can still be seen left at the base of the stone pillars.

101 1890. The decorated gate at Glanusk Park to welcome the Duke of Clarence.

102 *c*.1900. Crickhowell Volunteers on a church parade walking across the river Usk bridge.

103 The proclamation of George V—1910. Outside the market hall.

104 1910. Coronation festivities for George V. Marching down Beaufort Street. The scouts are leading the volunteers.

105 1914/15. Troops in the High Street. It is interesting to see the stone tiles on the outbuildings of Latham House, and the steel bars on the butcher's shop window.

106 Lord Glanusk addressing the troops before they leave for the front, 1914/18 war.

107   Troops, 1914/18 war. Before leaving for the front.

108   Signalling section. A large camp was situated at Talymaes, Llanbedr.

109   A funeral procession. Trailing the Arms down New Road 1914.

110   His Royal Highness the Duke of Windsor, addressing the people at the monument 1925.

111 His Royal Highness the Duke of Windsor at Glanusk Park 1925 with a shooting party.
Left to right: Back Row
Miss Lisle, Honar Phillips, Major Hon. Piers Leigh, Lord Digby, Lord Glanusk, Capt. I. Coates, James Edwards.
Front Row
Lady Digby, Lady Amy Coates, Mrs. Beckworth-Smith, Lady (Vera) Glanusk, His Royal Highness the Duke of Windsor, Mrs. Shonbridge, Lady Cara Aga and Major Beckworth-Smith.

112 The Bear Hotel decorated for the coronation of George VI.

113 Celebrations at Llangattock for the coronation of His Royal Highness George VI coronation.

114 Llanbedr Road, 1953. Street party celebrations for the coronation of Her Royal Highness Queen Elizabeth II.

Transport

115 Chauffeur-driven car outside the Clarence Hall in 1902. The car had solid wheels and wooden brake blocks.

116 1906. G.W.R. charabanc travelling from Crickhowell to Abergavenny railway station.

117 1913. Taking timber from Talymaes to Abergavenny. The driver Bill Randall and sitting on the top is Cyril Jones. Standing are Arthur Nolan, Bill Preece and Ron Leonard. Mr. Benjamin Watkins, The Wharf, Llangattock was the haulage contractor.

118 His Royal Highness the Duke of Windsor's Rolls Royce 1925. The Duke is stepping into the car after addressing the people from the monument.

119   1909. Charabanc owned by G.W.R. Sat beside the driver is Mr. Tommy Allen.

120   Scouts leaving Glanusk park for the International Jamboree in Birmingham c.1910. Lord Glanusk is looking on, there are four types of transport in the picture—Horse, Charabanc, Bus and Car.

121   Early c 1890. A horse-drawn carriage outside Pendre Cottage, Brecon Road.

122   1905. G.W.R. Bus. It is said that it cost a large amount of sixpenny's to travel to Abergavenny. The bus is picking up outside "Evans" the Carriers. The conductor is standing next to Mr. Evans. Most deliveries were made at this point

123 1904. Chauffeur for Lord Glanusk taken outside Glanusk Park.

124 Early c.1900 Donkey versus bus.

125   1912. The Abergavenny bus outside Crickhowell Post office.

126   This grand car was photographed by the Castle early c.1900. Driven by Mr. Tom Lewis (Auctioneer) His son is looking on.

127 1911. Motor bikes outside the Clarence Hall. The photograph shows *(left to right)* Dr.
Townley, Mr. Powell, Mr. & Mrs. T. J. Allen, Mr. Morris (Ironmonger), unknown person, Val
Jones (Haulier), Mr. Dart (Estate Agent for Dan-y-Parc House).

128 This accident happened at Pengenffordd 1920. The driver was Jack Barber. His son managed
to shut down before they were badly scaulded. They were hauling bricks to Talgarth.

129 Mr. T. J. Allen who was known as The Wizard. He was a local photographer, watch maker, jeweller, hairdresser, gunsmith, cycle and motor cycle agent, not to forget optical repairs. This photograph of him was taken in 1886 on his tricycle.

130 c.1900 Taken outside the Clarence Hall. A good form of transport, known as a Sulky.

131 1911. The photograph was taken outside the caretaker's house at the Clarence Hall.

132 c.1920. Mr. Wilks and his men in his garage which used to be at the top of New Road where now stands a petrol station.

133 1930. Mr. Gronway Jones at his garage in Beaufort Street, known as Castle Garage. The photograph shows a badly smashed-up car brought in from a road accident. Looking on are Mr Gronway Jones, Dennis Jones, Ron Leonard and Mr. W. C. Poulton.

134 1925. Mr. Tom Watkins, Haulage Contractor. This photograph shows one of his horses and carts.

135   1928. The River Usk was diverted with sandbags for the repair of the weir; stone sets were used weighing approximately 5cwt. The photograph shows A. J. Addis, Builders, commissioned to do the work. At one time a flood came and washed away the equipment, it ended up at Llangrwyney. The ledgers are still available for the work carried out and include 4 Ton of cement £14.4s.0d. a lorry and one man for a day £1.5s.0d., 3 loads of sand weighing 2 ton 14cwt £1.12s.8½d.

136   1887. The reservoir at Ffynnonau being built. It now feeds the lower end of Crickhowell.

137 In this photograph 1912, a road repair gang: Bill Randall, Mr. Batchelor and George Jones.

138 1912. Watching the road gang at work from her sidecar is Jessie Allen.

Sport

139 1904/5. Crickhowell A.F.C.

140 1920/21. Llangattock A.F.C. Mr. Bill Boddy is holding the ball.

141 1892. Crickhowell Cycle Club. The photograph was taken outside the house opposite Cwrt-y-Gollen. Mr. A. J. Addis is standing at the back. He won the 50 mile road race in 1893. The cup is still in Mr. John Addis's possession.

142 Crickhowell R.F.C. 1893.

Top left to right—F. Blocker, W. Prosser, A. J. Addis, T. Owen, and G. Jones.
Middle—T. Meale (Secretary), J. Jones, W. Johnson, W. Walking, J. Morgan and Mr. R. Loam.
3rd Row—J. Williams, M. Thomas, D. Evans and C. Thomas.
Front—D. R. Morgan and W. Batty.

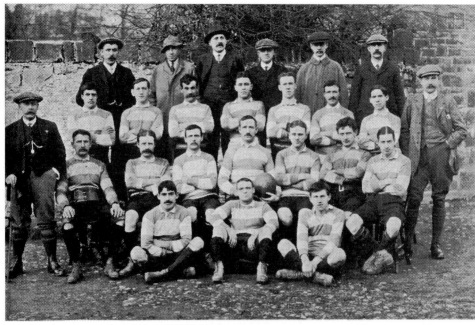

143 Crickhowell R.F.C. 1912/13. I have managed to name some of them.
Back row——3rd left Bill Townsend and 5th left Bill Gwenlam.
Second row——1st left Mr. Giles and second from right Alf Millet
Sitting——3rd left Charlie Leonard
Front row——Middle Harry Thompson.

144 1886/87. Committee members on the front of a fixture card. Inside some of the teams are——
Abergavenny Hearts of Oak, Christ College Brecon, Victoria and Waunlwyd, Ebbw Vale and
Blaenavon.

Members are reminded that all Subscriptions must be paid not later than the 1st November.

Any Donations, which may be sent to the Secretary, will be most thankfully received by him on behalf of the Club.

I. BLENNERHASSETT, *Hon. Sec.*

Ground——"The Old Cricket Field."

Subscriptions: Seniors, 2/-; Juniors, 1/-

Season 1886-87.

Crickhowell Football Club.

President:

E. M. WHITTING, ESQ.

Vice-Presidents.

REV. T. J. BOWEN, J. A. DOYLE, ESQ.,
A. E. JONES, ESQ., W. W. WEST, ESQ.

Captain.	*Vice-Captain.*
B. WATKINS.	W. JONES.

Committee.

R. PRICE	P. HARRINGTON	W. RUMSEY
W. DAVIES	D. SAUNDERS	A. EVANS

SECOND XV.

Captain.	*Vice-Captain.*
E. PRICE.	F. DAVIES.

Committee.

E. PRICE	C. VAUGHAN	R. EVANS

W. Rumsey, *Hon. Treasurer.*
I. Blennerhassett, *Hon. Sec.*

145 Crickhowell A.F.C. after winning the Brecon and District League.

146 The same side cleaned up for this photograph.

147 The photograph shows St. Edmunds School Football Club in 1920/21. In the photograph are Don Wallace, Ron Leonard, Jack Wilks and John Clements.

148 1930. Taken outside St. Edmunds School House, after winning the table tennis tournament. The Rev. Wilkinson and Mr. Lindsey are standing at the back. Also in the photograph is Mr. Bryn Meale—bottom second from left.

149 Crickhowell A.F.C. 1920 Committee members after winning the cup—Daff Morgan, Mr. Bufton, I. Huxley, Mr. Jones, Mark Day, Mr. H. Jones, C. Wallace, Unknown, Harry Huxley and Mr. H. Lovesey.

150 Crickhowell A.F.C. 1920 Cup winning team—*Top*—Unknown, Jim Wait and Patsy Griffiths
Middle—Fred Huxley, Bill Gray and Jim Huxley
Front—H. Parson, Dai George, Harold Jones, Ivor Huxley and Jim Bush.

151 1936. Who would have believed that we had a swimming club? The photo shows the diving board at the Galvey Meadow on the Usk, just above the Bullpit Meadow.

152 The front of a programme in 1936 which cost 2d in old money.

153 Malcolm Lloyd (Willie) who lived at the Dragon Hotel, undefeated Welsh Light Weight Champion 1956. Retired at 23 years of age. Reached number 8 in the Commonwealth ratings, most famous fights were with Dave Charnley holder of the British and European Empire titles. Willie beat him once, drew once and lost the title fight.

154 1928. A view inside the snooker room at Crickhowell Working Men's Club now a Conservative Club. A large house used to stand on the same site.

155 1930. A Race Meeting held at Ty-Rash Meadow. Seen here are—Mr. Kirkland, Rees Morgan, Colin Hudson, Ted Price and Dan Griffiths. Dan used to keep the Britannia Inn. On the right, holding a pint of beer, is Mr. Lovesey.

156 1949/50. Some of our mountains are excellent for rock climbing, here we can see some of our mountaineers. In the photograph are Bobby Sandeman and Louis Hurley.

157 1920. Crickhowell Bowls Club laying the first sod for the new green at Brecon Road ground, opposite the Old British School. On his knees is W. Lewis (Captain) on the right and also on his knees is T. J. Allen.

158 1920. The cricket field in the photograph is now the football field

159 Crickhowell Cricket Club 1950s
Back—C. Osborne, D. Osborne, W. Saunders, D. V. P. Lewis, G. Gabe, R. Maggs and Maj. Reynolds.
Front—W. T. Lloyd, Unknown, G. Hanson, J. Brittain, Unknown and G. Jenkins.

160 A late 1950s side.
Back—T. Carr, G. Gabe, Unknown, S. Clarke and T. Rodwell
Front—Unknown, D. Jehu, L. Jones, T. Williams and P. Saunders

161 Crickhowell Tennis Club's ground used to be at the end of the Elvicta football pitch. The team in the photograph were undefeated champions of 1922.

162 Another team photograph of 1923.

163 1898. This fine gentleman sat under the bridge was known as John Moonlight. By his side is a rod and a salmon which must weigh a good 20lb.

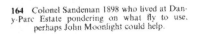

164 Colonel Sandeman 1898 who lived at Dan-y-Parc Estate pondering on what fly to use, perhaps John Moonlight could help.

165 and 166   Some of the runners on their way to the
Empire Games held in Cardiff in 1958. They were greeted
by Sir William L. Parker, Bart, Lord Lieutenant of
Breconshire, Councillor J. Mills-Price, Chairman of
Crickhowell Rural District Council and Mr. Fred
Foster, Clerk, look on.

167 1910. Ernest King, Game Keeper at Glanusk Estate and his wife standing outside the lodge.

168 1910. Scene of shooters having a well-earned break. Ernest King is sat in the middle. His father was also game keeper to Lord Glanusk. He was murdered in 1876 by poachers; the wood where it happened is called King's wood after him.

169   1907. Crickhowell Harriers meet at Bellfountain wood.

170   A meet at the Bear Hotel 1920. The Kennels in those days were at Oak Road.

171 Rifle Club 1920. In this photograph are—W. V. Jones, T. J. Allen, J. Powell, W. Davies and H. Jenkins.

172 Another team of Crickhowell Rifle Club. In the back row second from left is Reg Sharman.

173 Local Sheep Dog trials 1920.

174 1910. Washing the sheep at Glanusk. The lodge can be seen on the left.

Schools

175 The British school 1890.

176 Llangynidr School 1900.

177   British School, Brecon Road

Back left to right — Peggy Gow, Joan King, Gwyneth Hughes, Beatrice Lewis and Lilian Jones
Front — Bert Price, Leonard Chatworthy, David Morgan, Doug Millett, John Ralph, T. H. Thomas (Headteacher);

178 Llangattock School 1910.

179 St. Edmunds School, Crickhowell 1930. Some of the pupils are
Front Row——Tom Edwards, George Beavis, Richard Beavis, Georgina Ravenill, Monica Maggs,
Barbara Lewis, Jean Watkeys, Velma Werret, Russell Jones, Joslyn Edwards and John Morgan.
Second Row——John Meredith, Glenys Addis, Beryl Clarke, Trevor Addis, Mary Clarke, Barbara
Lewis, Lilian Watkeys, Gladys Whitney, Gwen Jones and Ken Hester.
Top Row——John Morgan, Colin Meredith, Jim Whitney and Reg Goody.

People and Entertainment

180 Around the maypole at a garden party at Glanyrafon 1910.

181 A day out on the Table Mountain was quite common in 1913. Here we see the Allen family enjoying themselves.

182 A typical wedding in 1890. A. J. Addis marries Rose Thomas.

183 and 184 c.1900. Some wonderful times, on a day's outing when almost everybody went on school trips on the canal.

185 The House Party, Glanusk Park, Breconshire, September 18th, 1890. Those present were Mr. Bailey, Mrs. Bailey, Miss Marjory Bailey, J. Launcelot Bailey, Lady Bailey, H.R.H. the Duke of Clarence & Avondale, Miss Gwladys Bailey, Viscountess Emlyn, The Hon. Mrs. Wood, The Right Hon. Viscount Cross, K.C.B., Miss Bailey, Miss Llewelyn, Miss Edith Bailey, Sir J. R. Bailey, Bart., M.P., Sir J. D. Llewelyn, Bart., Lady Llewelyn, Viscount Emlyn, The Hon. Georgina Cross, The Hon. Edith Campbell, T. Wood, Esq., H. Fripp, Esq. and Herbert Bailey

186 Concert party c.1900. Mr. Val Jones is on the right.

187 A church party at Llangattock 1930.

188 St. Edmunds Band of Hope 1890.

189 *c.*1900. Scout camp at Glanusk.

190 Scout Jamboree at Glanusk Park. Beside the Fish Stone. Lord Glanusk was the 1st Chief Commissioner for the scouts in Wales.

191 This fine-looking room was the Club House for the Beaufort Arms. Now Castle Garage stands there.

192 1920. Some of the young actors in the Band of Hope outside the Clarence Hall.

193 1910. Society of Odd Fellows outside the Corn Exchange.

194 Bethesda, Llangattock. Some of the people in the photograph are—Elsie Tranter, Gladys Palliser, Doris Morgan, Mrs. Williams, Kate Games, Dulcie Games, D. Bevan, Myra Wills, E. Lewis, M. Gwen, Mrs. Worthing, Minister of Bethesda, and Wilfred Williams.

195 T. J. Allen 1893 known as the "Wizard". He was the local photographer who took most of the photographs in this book. Some glass plates are still in existence and were developed for the book.

196 c.1950. Two of Crickhowell's well known characters, Mr Kirkland, the chemist, and Malcolm Paton sitting outside the chemist shop

197 The first Lord Glanusk with some of his children.

198 The second and third Lord Glanusk,
Wilfred Russell and Joseph Russell.

199   1905. Llangattock Park Workers.

200   1920. Glanusk Park Workers.

201 c.1900. The Agricultural Show, which was held in the field by the Industrial Estate as you enter Crickhowell from Abergavenny on the A40

202 c.1900. One of the many Garden Parties held at Glan Nant.

203 c.1920. Sergeant Morgan Lewis and P.C. Tom Lewis (Father & Son) This photograph shows them outside the Old Police Station, New Road. On his retirement Sergeant Lewis was presented with a leather chair by the people of Crickhowell

204 Crickhowell Special Police 1940.

205 Crickhowell Home Guard 1940.

206 Llangattock Home Guard 1940.

207   Crickhowell Volunteers 1914.

208   Crickhowell Volunteer Fire Brigade 1971—
Back—D. J. Addis, T. Lloyd, P. Witherstone, J. Preece, R. Williams and R. Jones.
Front—R. Evans, B. Couzens, Chief Fire Officer Faulkner and G. Games.

210 Mr. Trevor Addis, local builder who at the age of 76 rebuilt the church porch at St. Edmunds church. On his death locals made a collection and placed a seat outside the Corn Exchange Inn in memory of him

209 c.1928. Standing outside her cottage on the Legar. Mrs. Addis holding her daughter. The face of the cottage has changed quite a lot.

211   c.1950. Some of Crickhowell's well known citizens: on the right Lord Brecon, Sid Davies, T. J. Allen and Colonel Rees.

212   1963. A crowd of people waiting the arrival of Queen Elizabeth II and Prince Philip who came to open the Welsh Brigade Depot at Cwrt-y-Gollen.

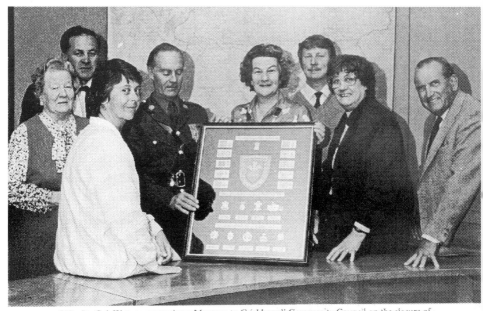

213 Lt. Col. Watson presenting a Montage to Crickhowell Community Council on the closure of Cwrt-y-Gollen Army Camp in 1986.
Left to Right—Mrs. B. Games, L. Watts, Mrs. S. Fletcher (Clerk), Lt. Col. Watson, Mrs. A. Usborne (Chairman), Mr. D. J. Addis, Mrs. J. Pratley and Dr. G. Herdman.

214 Mrs. Thatcher who visited Crickhowell Conservative Club in 1977. In the picture are:
Left to Right—Mrs. A. Usborne, Dennis Thatcher, Lady Kitson, Mrs. Thatcher, Jack Price and Mr. Trevor Evans.

215 1977. P.C. Stan Austin. A well known policeman in Crickhowell. Here we see Stan opening the door for Mrs. Thatcher when she visited Crickhowell. This was before she was Prime Minister.

216 After raising £1,000 for diabetic research it was presented to the great artiste "Sir Harry Secombe" by local fundraisers. In the photograph: *Left to Right*—Mrs. H. Waring, Mrs. P. Brabner, Sir Harry Secombe, Mrs. C. Roberts, Mrs. A. Usborne and Mrs. S. Addis.

Snow and Floods

217 The snows of 1982 caused a rush to stock up on bread. Here we see a queue of people outside the bakers.

218 1982. Snow. Bridge Street completely blocked off.

219 1931. Floods in Bridge Street.
A boat is used to rescue some of the people.

220 1931. Floods in Bridge Street.
Residents look on

221   1962 Floods.
Looking on by the turning to Llangattock

222   The old garage at New Road. Now Business Offices

223 1979. Glangrwyney to Gilwern Road, washed away.
A car washed over the side, the small boy is author's son John.

224 1979. The Arches to the River Bridge were completely blocked
with trees and rubbish causing the flood to build up even more.
The Bailey Bridge on the right was put there when urgent repairs were
needed to the Old Bridge. It now stands on the road between Gilwern
and Llangrwyney.

225 1880. Looking down Beaufort Street before Council Offices were built.